World History
in Pictures

World History in Pictures

BY PETER ILSØE
AND OLUF JONSEN

SECOND EDITION REVISED AND ENLARGED

GEORGE G. HARRAP & CO. LTD

LONDON · TORONTO · WELLINGTON

SYDNEY

First published in Great Britain 1965
by GEORGE G. HARRAP & CO. LTD
182 High Holborn, London W.C. 1
Second Edition Revised and Enlarged 1968
© *Gyldendalske Boghandel, Nordisk Forlag A.S.* 1963
English translation © *George G. Harrap & Co. Ltd.* 1964, 1968
Printed in Denmark 1968.

PREFACE

World History in Pictures has in view the grammar school sixth form, teachers' training colleges, and corresponding levels.

The material is mainly arranged chronologically, but regard has had to be paid to colour plates and to the general format, which means that departures from historical sequence may occur.

We have dealt not only with political history, but also, in the broadest sense, with cultural history. We have tried to use pictures which illustrate specific subjects – agriculture, industry and crafts, transport, architecture – through the centuries. Also pictures illustrating life in all parts of the world have been included. Modern times have relatively the highest number of pictures (about 150).

Some of the pictures will be familiar, others are not so well known. Our aim has been to choose those that we consider are significant in the cultural tradition of western Europe.

We have in many instances placed pictures together when their juxtaposition is reciprocally illuminating – different portraits of the same person (214 and 215; 232, 233, and 234; 264 and 265; 272 and 273; 345 and 346; and others); different portrayals of the same event (303 and 304); different reproductions in a related field (22 and 23; 244 and 245); different pictures of social types, characteristic of different periods (266 and 267) and countries (310 and 312); and, finally, representations of conditions in the same field at different periods (289 and 290; 403 and 404; 405 and 406; 411 and 412; 415 and 416).

At the end of the book we have placed plans of buildings and towns which will probably be useful for reference.

The Editors

NOTE TO THE SECOND ENGLISH EDITION

This edition contains twenty-six new pictures which were included in the second and third Danish editions. Ten of these (68, 80b, 81a, 81c, 83a, 108, 227b, 227c, 259b, and 259c) relate to the period covered by the first edition; the remaining sixteen (411, 412, 413, 414, and 417–428) bring the book up to date. Seven illustrations (17, 18, 64a, 92, 186, 364, and 400) have been replaced by others with the same motif, while in many cases further information has been added to the descriptions of the pictures. Finally, the content of the book has been increased by the addition of fourteen ground-plans (2, 3, 8a, 10a, 10b, 11, 12, 14, 16, 20, 21, 22, 23, and 24) and two reconstructions (4 and 9b).

The purpose of these changes and additions is to improve the book still further for foundation work in visual education at high schools and training colleges. This we have tried to do principally by obtaining material to illustrate many facets of the same subject.

The Editors

1. Bison licking its flank. Carved on reindeer horn in relief. Musée des Antiquités, Saint-Germain-en-Laye. From La Madeleine, Tursac, Dordogne. 20,000–15,000 B.C. Base of horn to muzzle, 36 mm.

3. Flint knife with carved handle in ivory from Gebel-el-Arak, Egypt. 3500–3200 B.C. Length, 28 cm. Louvre, Paris.

2. Flint dagger from Hindsgavl region of Funen (Fyn), Denmark. 1800–1500 B.C. Length, 29 cm. National Museum, Copenhagen.

4. Bronze statuette of warlike deity with four eyes and arms. Sardinia. First millennium B.C.
Height, 21.5 cm. The Museum in Cagliari.

5. Stonehenge, Salisbury Plain, England. *c.* 1900–1400 B.C. Seen from the north-east (see groundplan No. 1).

6. Wizard on rock engraving on promontory at Lake Onega, East Finland. Pre-Roman Iron Age. Height, 52 cm.

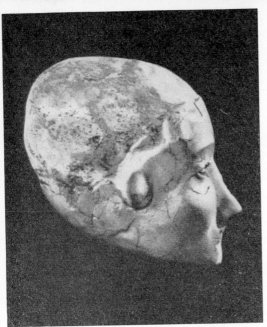

7. Modelled features on skull from Jericho.
Sixth millennium B.C. British Museum.

8. Foundation of houses
in ancient Jericho.
Sixth millennium B.C.

9. Farming scene. Wall painting from Sennezem's tomb in Thebes. Height, approximately 1 m.
c. 1300 B.C.

2*

10. The pyramid of Cheops
and the Sphinx at Gizeh.
Limestone. *c.* 2600 B.C.
Height of pyramid,
143.5 m. Height of Sphinx,
approximately 20 m.;
length approximately 60 m.
(see groundplan No. 2).

11. Part of the Temple of Horus, Edfu. The best preserved temple of ancient Egypt. *c.* 200 B.C.
Height of gate towers, 35 m. (see groundplan No. 3).

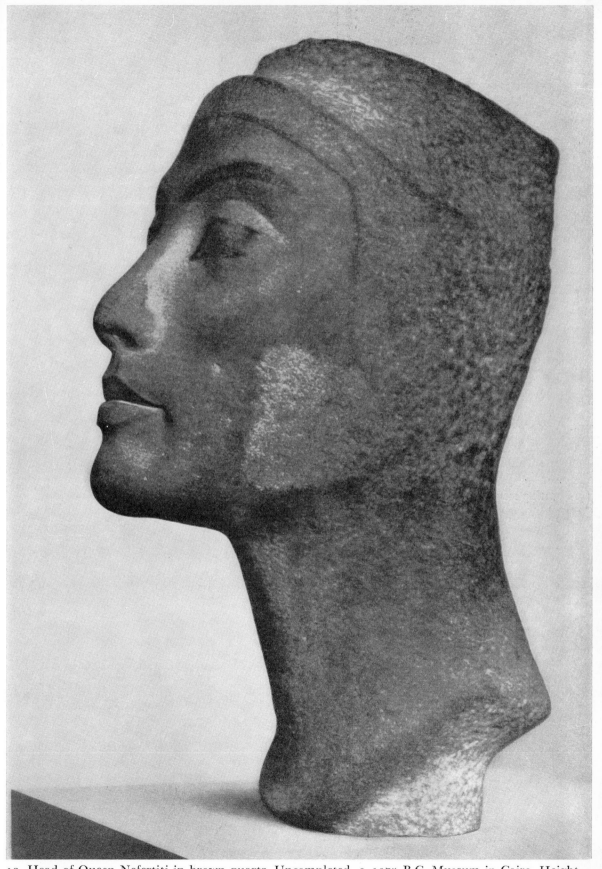

12. Head of Queen Nefertiti in brown quartz. Uncompleted. *c.* 1375 B.C. Museum in Cairo. Height, 33 cm.

13. Rameses II. Head of giant
statue at the Temple of Ptah,
Memphis. 1300 B.C. Height,
full statue, 13 m.

14. Hunting scene. Wall painting from grave of Mena (Narmer), Thebes. *c.* 1420 B.C. Height, 75 cm.

15. The weighing of the heart against the feather of truth. From *The Book of the Dead (Ani Papyrus)*. Height, 27 cm., length, 56 cm. *c.* 1450 B.C. British Museum.

16. Milking and dairy scene. Limestone frieze from temple in El Obeid. Height, 22 cm. Background, black slate. Copper frame. Beginning of third millennium B.C. Baghdad Museum.

17. Ziggurat in Ur. A ziggurat is an Assyrian or Babylonian temple tower in which each storey is smaller than the one below it. Built in brick. *c.* 2100 B.C. Length, approximately 60 m., breadth, approximately 45 m. (see groundplan No. 4).

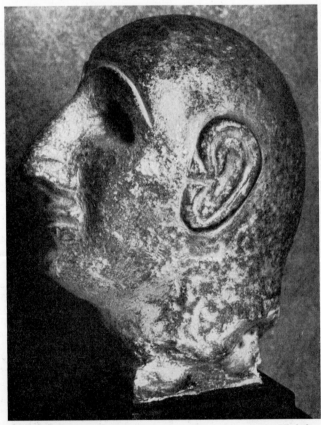

18. Sumerian head. Limestone. 3000–2500 B.C. Height, 7 cm. Louvre.

19. King Hammurabi and the Sun God. Upper part of a stele with a relief, below which is the text of Hammurabi's laws. Diorite stele: height, 2.25 m. Relief: height, 65 cm. *c.* 1700 B.C. Louvre.

20. King Tiglath-pileser (745–727 B.C.) attacks a fortified town. Relief in alabaster from Nimrud near Nineveh. Height, 96 cm. British Museum.

21. Schoolroom (13 m. x 8 m.) in the palace at Mari. Seen from the north-east. *c.* 1800 B.C.

22. King Assur-bani-pal's horses are led to his hunting chariot. Alabaster relief from his palace at Nineveh. Height, 50 cm. *c.* 650 B.C. British Museum.

23. Hittite war chariot in battle. Mural relief, Jerablus-Karkamis. *c.* 800 B.C. Archaeological Museum, Ankara.

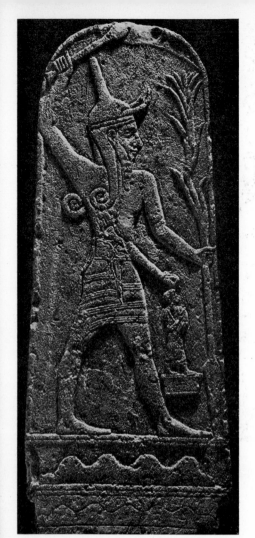

24. Limestone stele of a deity from Ugarit (Ras Shamra) in Northern Syria. Height, 1.42 m. Thirteenth to twelfth century B.C. Louvre.

25. Limestone bust of woman, probably a goddess, from Elche, Spain. Height, 53 cm. Fifth to fourth century B.C. Museo Archeologico, Madrid.

26. The large reservoir in the castle at Mohenjo Daro, Indus Valley. 2500–1500 B.C.

27a. Fragment of earthen vessel showing zebu. From the Indus culture. Found at Abu-Dhabi, on an island in the Persian Gulf. 2500–2000 B.C.

27b. Sumerian stone seal with harp player from the island of Failaka, off Kuwait. 2500–2000 B.C.

28. King Darius and the rebel prisoners. Relief sculptured on a cliff-face at Behistan.
Darius, 1.73 m. high. Length of relief, 5.50 m. *c.* 520 B.C.

29. Darius gives an audience. Behind him is the heir to the throne, Xerxes. Relief from the palace at
Persepolis, approximately 6.22 m. wide. *c.* 500 B.C.

30. One wing of the double stairway at the entrance to the throne-room (*apadana*) in the palace of Darius, Persepolis. Columns, approximately 18 m. high. *c.* 500 B.C.

31. Outside staircase (right) to the main entrance of the palace with audience stairs (left). Phaistos, Crete. *c.* 1650–1400 B.C.

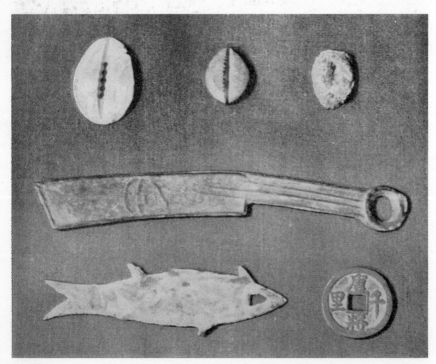

32. The 'money' of Ancient China. (1) Imitation cowrie shell of 1000 B.C.
(2) Bronze 'coin' in the form of a knife (13.8 cm. long), first century B.C.
(3) Bronze 'coin' as fish (8.8 cm. long). First millennium B.C. (4) Bronze coin from 200 B.C. This type of money was in use until around 1900 A.D.

33. The Lion Gate, Mycenae. Breadth of gate opening, 3.07 m. *c.* 1300 B.C.

34. Gold coin (stater) from Lydia, struck under King Croesus (561–546 B.C.). (2 : 1). Nationalmuseet, Copenhagen.

35. Restored impression of a seal showing bull-jumping, from Cnossos. Diameter, 3 cm. Crete. *c.* 1550–1530 B.C.

36. Gold ring (bevelled), found at Mycenae, showing warriors in battle. 1550–1400 B.C. (Illustrating *The Iliad.*) Diameter, 3.4 cm. National Museum, Athens.

37. Smithy. Sketch from black-figured vase painting from the last quarter of the sixth century B.C. Boston Museum.

38. Greek vase painting. King Arcesilas II (*c.* 570-568 B.C.) supervises the weighing and dispatch of the medicinal herb silphium from Cyrene, North Africa. *c.* 560 B.C. Bibliothèque Nationale, Paris.

39. Greek vase painting. Red-figured Attic krater, showing young men training with the discus and weights. Fifth century B.C. Villa Giulia, Rome.

40. Greek warriors set out with war chariot. Relief from base of statue. 85 cm. wide. *c.* 500 B.C. National Museum, Athens.

41. Hermes with one of the three Graces on a relief found on Thasos. 83 cm. wide. Close of sixth century B.C. Louvre.

42. Athene, by Myron.
c. 450 B.C. Roman copy
in marble. 1.73 m. high.
State Museum at Frankfurt-
am-Main.

43. Greek vase painting of girls bathing, by the Andokides Painter. *c.* 530 B.C. Louvre.

44. Poseidon, Apollo, and Artemis. Relief from the Panathenaic frieze, east end of the Parthenon. Height, 1.06 m. *c.* 440 B.C. Acropolis Museum, Athens.

5. The building known as the Temple of Poseidon (Temple of Hera), *c.* 450 B.C.; and the Basilica, *c.* 540 B.C. Roman road in the foreground. Paestum, southern Italy (see groundplan No. 5).

6. Attic vase painting. Ancient Greek merchant ship. Late sixth century B.C. British Museum.

47. The theatre and the Temple of Apollo at Delphi. Fourth century B.C.

48. The theatre at Epidaurus in the Peloponnese. *c.* 350 B.C.

49. The Acropolis as seen from the Pnyx, Athens.

50. The Parthenon, built 447–432 B.C. Seen from the north-west.

51. South-western part of the agora (market-place), Athens, after recent excavations.

52. Reconstructed model of the agora.

53. Terracotta statuette of a school-
boy on his way home with school
satchel. Tanagra figurine. Height, 16 cm.
National Museum, Athens.

54. Marble statuette of Socrates.
Roman copy of Greek original
of the fourth century B.C. Height,
27.5 cm. British Museum.

55. Alexander the Great in battle. Mosaic floor from Pompeii, probably from the second century B.C., from a third-century painting. Length, 5.12 m. National Museum, Naples.

56. Silver phalera with military elephant. Early Hellenic, Syrian, or Bactrian work. The Hermitage, Leningrad.

57. The peristyle in the house of Dionysus at Delos. Seen from the south. Second century B.C. (see groundplan No. 6).

8. The street of tombs, Cervetri. Etruscan. *c.* 500 B.C.

59. Interior of the family vault of the Matunas. "The Tomb of the Reliefs" in Cervetri. *c.* 300 B.C.

51. Sarcophagus of Laris Pulenas from "The Tomb of the Magistrate" at Tarquinia. *c.* 300 B.C.
Museum, Tarquinia.

62. Marble relief of a Roman soldier and his family. Found near Rome. *c.* 50 B.C. Length 2.05 m.
Boston Museum.

63 a. Marble head of Caesar. *c.* 100 A.D. Height, 95 cm. National Museum, Naples.

64 a. Marble head of Pompey. Height, 25 cm Copy from the time of Claudius. Ny Carlsberg Glyptotek, Copenhagen.

63 b. Silver coin (denarius) with Caesar's head (2 : 1). 44 B.C.

64 b. Silver coin (denarius) with Pompey's head. (2 : 1). 38 B.C.

65 a. Vespasian. Contemporary marble head. Height, 39 cm. Ny Carlsberg Glyptotek, Copenhagen.

66. Augustus as High
Priest. *c.* 10 A.D. Marble.
Height, 2.05 m. Museo
delle Terme, Rome.

65 b. Copper coin (sestert) with
Vespasian's head. Struck 71 A.D.
Diameter, 3.2 cm.

65 c. Silver tetradrachme with
Cleopatra's head. *c.* 35 B.C.
Diameter, 2.6 cm.

67. The Mamertine underground prison called the Tullianum in Rome. Rebuilt under Sulla.

68. A sleeping slave boy.
Roman work from a Greek
original. Museo delle Terme,
Rome.

69. The house of the Vettii at Pompeii. Peristyle and garden. Seen from the south. Middle of first
century A.D. (see groundplan No. 8 b).

70. Strada dell' Abbondanza, Pompeii. Reconstructed impression of north side.

71. Piazzale delle Corporazioni, Ostia. *c.* 200 A.D. Eastern portion.

72. *Thermopolium*, Ostia. Third century A.D. Restored.

73. *Latrine publici*, Ostia. Shops of the second century A.D. were converted to public lavatories in the fourth century, after the dividing walls had been removed.

4. *Triclinium* (the dining-room) at the Moralist's House, Pompeii. First century A.D. Seen from the south-west.

5. Flagstone floor *(lithostrotos)*, Antonia Castle, Jerusalem. From the time of Christ.

76. Via della Fontana, Ostia. *c.* 130 A.D. (see groundplans Nos. 9 a and 9 b).

78. Mithraic temple under San Clemente Church, Rome
Third century A.D. (see groundplan No. 14

77. Interior of the Pantheon, best preserved of the buildings of ancient Rome. Some restoration was undertaken in the eighteenth and nineteenth centuries, and the tombs are recent. Built by Hadrian. c. 125 A.D. Height, 43.3 m.

79. Colosseum, Rome. 80 A.D.

80 a. The Arch of Titus, Rome.
Shortly after 81 A.D.
Seen from the east.

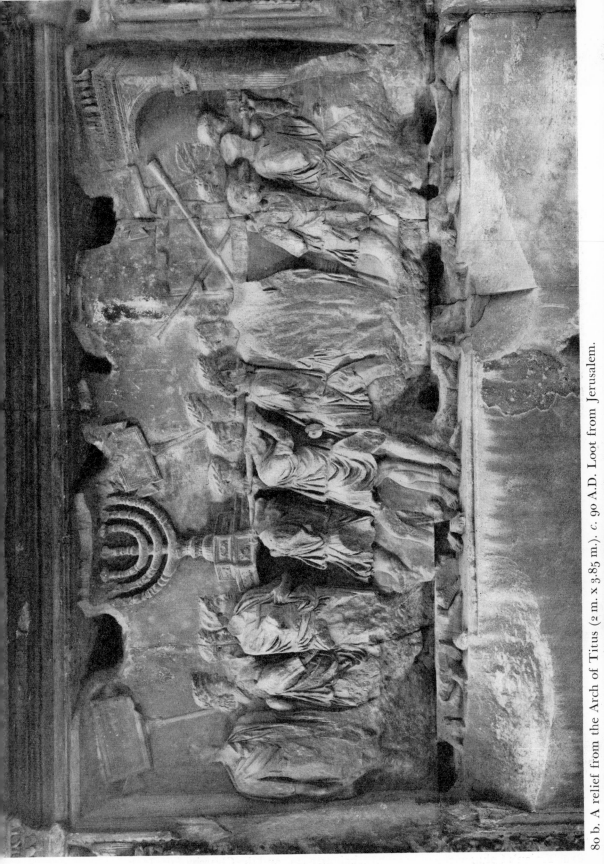

80 b. A relief from the Arch of Titus (2 m. x 3.85 m.). c. 90 A.D. Loot from Jerusalem.

81 a. Trajan's Column, erected 113 A.D., height, 38 m., and the Church of the Holy Name of Mary, Rome

81 b. Part of Trajan's Column. The lower bands of the spiral relief approximately 90 cm. high.

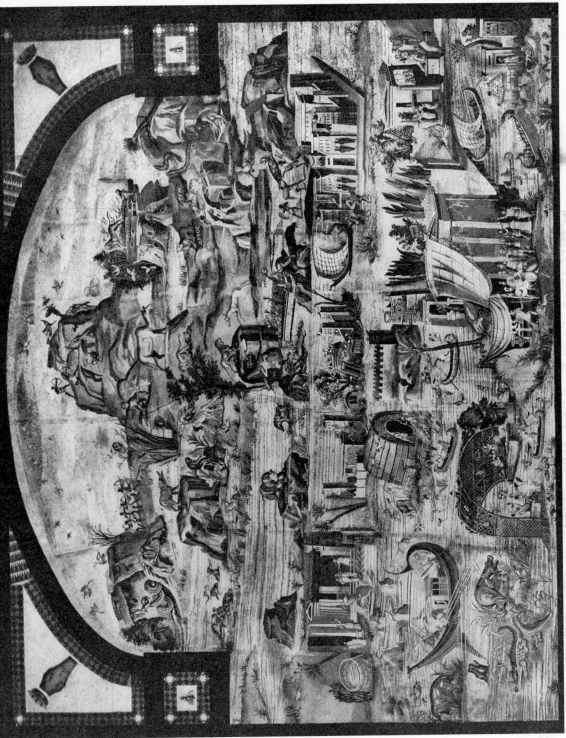

82. Mosaic with Egyptian themes. Palestrina, Italy. (6.56 x 5.25 m.). *c.* 80 B.C. Restored.

83 a. Upper storey of the shopping street (literally Bazaar Street) or the sales hall of Trajan's market, Rome. *c.* 100 A.D. (see groundplans Nos. 10 a and 10 b).

83 b. Trajan's market with medieval tower in the background. Rome. *c.* 100 A.D. (see groundplans Nos. 10 a and 10 b).

84. Equestrian statue of Marcus Aurelius on the Capitoline Hill, Rome. Height, 5.12 m. 176 A.D.

85. Giant head of Constantine
the Great. The head is 2.60 m.
high, and the eye is 30 cm. wide.
Marble. Palazzo dei Conservatori,
Rome. *c.* 315 A.D.

86. Part of the Baths of
Caracalla, Rome.
211–216 A.D.
(see groundplan No. 11).

7. The Forum Romanum seen from the Capitoline Hill.

FORO ROMANO VISTO DAL CAMPIDOGLIO

TEMPIO DEI CASTORI   PALATINO

CVRIA GIVLIA   BASILICA DI COSTANTINO COLOSSEO ARCO DI TITO BASILICA GIVLIA TEMPIO DI AVGVSTO

ARCO DI SETTIMIO SEVERO TEMPIO DI ANTONINO E FAVSTINA ARCO DI FABIO CASA DELLE VESTALI VIA SACRA TEMPIO DI SATVRNO

BASILICA EMILIA TABERNE TEMPIO DI GIVLIO CESARE TEMPIO DI VESTA ARCO DI TIBERIO

VMBILICVS ROMAE STATVA DI COSTANTINO-LAGO DI CVRZIO COLONNE ONORARIE

VVLCANALE ROSTRI COLONNA DI FOCA COLONNA MILIARIA

38. Reconstruction of the Forum Romanum. Seen from the Capitoline Hill.

89. Relief of chariot races (50 cm. x 1.25 m.) in the Circus Maximus, Rome. Close of third century. Museo Civico, Foligno.

90. The transport of wine on the Moselle. Relief in marble from a gravestone at Neumagen. *c.* 200 A.D. Length of ship about 3 m. Partly restored. The Museum at Trier.

1. Porta Nigra at Trier. *c.* 325 A.D. Tower is 29 m. high (see groundplan No. 12).
en from the north.

2. Aqueduct at Nimes (Pont du Gard), southern France. Height, approximately 50 m. Built under Augustus. Restored, 1855–59.

93. Round temple and the temple of Fortuna Virilis (*c.* 50 B.C.), in the
Forum Boarium (Cattle Market), Rome.

94. Hadrian's Wall, northern England. The wall is approximately 120 km. in length, with an average
height of 6–7 m. 122–131 A.D.

95. Roman villa (farmstead). Reconstruction. Chedworth, Gloucestershire. *c.* 300 A.D. (see groundplan No. 13).

96. Roman baths, main hall. First to third century A.D. Bath, England.

97. The theatre at Sabratha, Tripoli, North Africa. *c.* 200 A.D. Seen from the south-east.

98. Arles, southern France, showing the amphitheatre (136 m. long) and the theatre. First century A.D

99. Dockworker. Mosaic. Piazzale delle Corporazioni, Ostia. Second to third century A.D.

00. High official, accompanied by his bodyguard. Floor mosaic from the ancient palace, Piazza rmerina, Sicily. c. 300 A.D.

101. A catacomb, Rome.

102. Adelphia's sarcophagus. Length, 2.5 m. *c.* 350 A.D. Museo Nazionale, Syracuse.

103. Mosaic apse of the Church of Santa Pudenziana, Rome. *c.* 400 A.D. Right side much restored.

104. Santa Maria in Cosmedin, Rome. *c.* 500 A.D. Restored *c.* 800 A.D. (Compare with groundplan No. 14).

105. Interior of St Sophia, Istanbul. 532–537 A.D. The diameter of the main dome is 32.7 m., height, 55.6 m. (see groundplan No. 15).

106. Justinian with courtiers. Wall mosaic (2.7 m. x 4.1 m.) in the Church of San Vitale, Ravenna c. 550 A.D.

107. Helmet from Sutton Hoo, England. *c.* 650 A.D.
British Museum. Restored.

108. Equestrian statuette of
Carolingian king, possibly
Chartemagne. Bronze. Height
24 cm. Ninth century. Louvre.

99. The prayer book of St Boniface (*Ragyndrudis Codex*).
750 A.D. Cathedral Museum, Fulda, Hesse.

110. Charles the Bald with
monks from Tours.
Miniature from Charles the
Bald's Evangelistary.
c. 845 A.D. Bibliothèque
Nationale, Paris.

111. Interior of the palace chapel at Aachen Cathedral.
Looking towards the choir from the octagon. 796–804 A.D.
(see groundplan No. 16).

112. Part of English wooden church. Greenstead, Essex. Tenth century.

13. Ste Foy. Reliquary statuette. Tenth century. Conques, southern France.

114. The Kaabah in Mecca (12 x 10.5 x 10.5 m.) surrounded by colonnade and minarets.

115. Mohammedans at prayer. Changing prayer positions.

6. The Dome of the Rock (Mosque of Omar), Jerusalem. Seventh century.

7. The Sultan Ahmed (Ahmed I) Mosque, called the Blue Mosque, Istanbul. 1609–16. Obelisk, and twisted column from Delphi, in foreground (see groundplan No. 17).

118. Bayeux tapestry (70 m. x 50 cm.). The invasion fleet crossing the Channel. Late eleventh centur[y]
Bayeux Museum.

119. Bayeux tapestry. Battle scene with William the Conqueror to the right. Late eleventh century.
Bayeux Museum.

120. The Castle of Coucy (central tower, dungeon), Laon. *c.* 1230. Destroyed by German bombardment in 1917.

1. The Castle of the Counts, Ghent. Founded ninth or tenth century.

122. The Cathedral at Speyer.
Eleventh century.
Eastern section (see groundplan No. 18).

123. The cloisters of the Benedictine monastery of Monreale, Palermo. *c.* 1200.

124. The nave of the Madeleine church at Vézelay.
1120-30.

125. St Bernard of Clairvaux.
Miniature by Jean Fouquet.
c. 1450. Musée Condé, Chantilly.

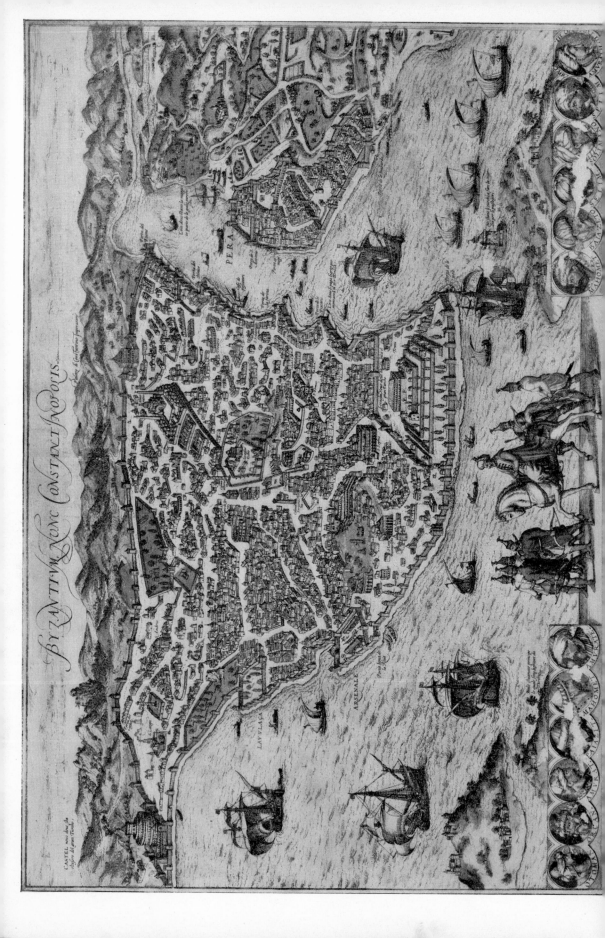

BYZANTIVM NVNC CONSTANTINOPOLIS

26. Constantinople, from *Theatrum urbium,* by Braunius. 1572.

27. Jerusalem's north wall – the part of the wall which Godfrey de Bouillon breached in 1099.

128. Krak des Chevaliers. Crusaders' castle at the crossing of trade-routes in Syria. Twelfth to thirteenth century. Seen from the north-west.

129. The Court of the Myrtles and Comares Tower, Alhambra, Granada. Fourteenth
century.

130. (a) Dispensing spiritual
and worldly endowments
(enfeoff with fiefs).
(b) The law of the land and
excommunication by the Church
is fulfilled. Miniature from
Sachsenspiegel. c. 1300.

131. Effigy of Rudolf I, founder of the Habsburg imperial dynasty. Speyer Cathedral. c. 1300.

2. Ste Chapelle, Paris. Upper Chapel. 1245–48.

133. Part of the Palace of the
Popes, Avignon. During the Great
Schism the rival Pope lived and
held his court here.
Engraving of 1618.

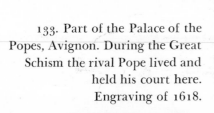

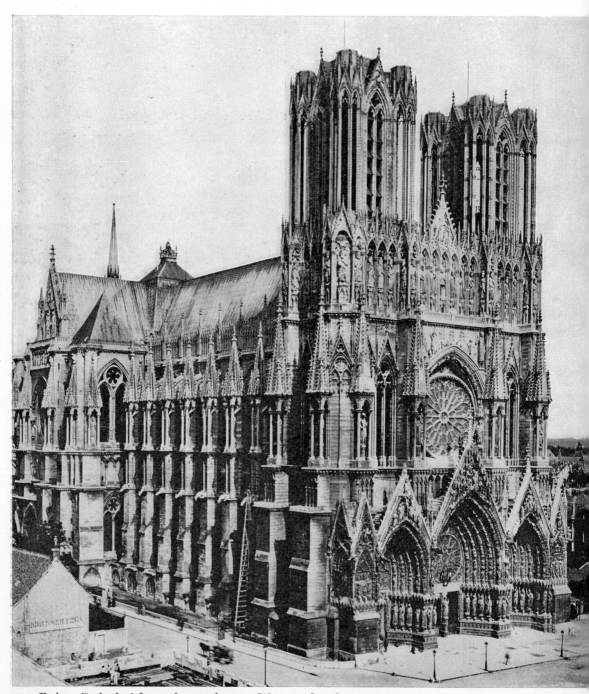

134. Reims Cathedral from the north-west. Western façade. 1231–90.

35. Reims Cathedral. Nave and choir. 1214–1428 (see groundplan No. 19).

136. Corpus Christi Day procession in St Mark's Square, Venice, by Gentile Bellini. 1496. Accademia, Venice.

137. Jean Miélot translates *The Miracles of Our Lady. c.* 1455. Bibliothèque Nationale, Paris.

138. Simon Nockaert presents to Philip the Good of Burgundy a translation of *Les Chroniques de Hainaut*, 1448. (The boy to the right of the Duke is Charles the Bold.) Bibliothèque Royale, Brussels.

139. Mystery play. "The Martyrdom of St Apollonia." From Jean Fouquet's *Heures d'Étienne Chevalier*. 1452–60. Musée Condé, Chantilly.

140. St Francis weds Lady Poverty. Fresco by Giotto in the Lower Church of St Francis in Assisi. *c.* 130

141. The body of the saint is cut into pieces (relics). Early twelfth century. Vatican Library.

2. A monk and a nun in the stocks. From *The Decretals of Gregory IX. c.* 1340. British Museum.

143. Monk drinking wine. Fourteenth century. Miniature, initial A. British Museum.

144. Watchman's gallery on the town walls, Rothenburg.
The walls date from 1200 to 1400.

145. The Castle of Eltz on
the Mosel. This has been in
the family's possession since
1517. The building dates
from the first half of the
thirteenth century to the
sixteenth century. It was
destroyed by fire in 1920,
but was rebuilt in its old form.

146. Central tower of a medieval castle – exterior and section.

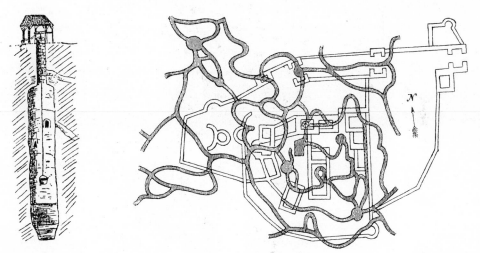

7. (a) Well in a castle with secret passages from the well-shaft. (b) System of underground
ssages beneath the Castle of Pottenstein in Bohemia.

148. Inside Nuremberg Castle, showing the well-house and high tower. The oldest part of the tower is medieval. The most recent part dates from 1561.

149. Harlech Castle, North Wales. Built by Edward I towards the end of the thirteenth century.

150. A tournament. Relief in ivory on a decorated casket. French work, 1330–50. Victoria and Albert Museum, London.

151. Investiture of a knight. Sword, shield, spurs, and helmet are received by the new knight. French miniature. Fourteenth century. Bibliothèque de l'Arsenal, Paris.

152. The Gardens of Love. Flemish miniature from *Roman de la Rose* (Renaud de Montauban).
c. 1490. Bibliothèque de l'Arsenal, Paris.

153. A banquet. Flemish miniature. *Les très riches heures du Duc de Berry. c.* 14»
Musée Condé, Chantill

154. Equestrian statue of the *condottiere* Gattamelata, by Donatello. 1447-53. Padua.

5. Sir Geoffrey Luttrell bids farewell to his wife and daughter-in-law. From the Luttrell Psalter. 1340. British Museum.

156. Siege of Swiss town, 1339. (Circle of wagons for defence, and a "tank.") Portion of a Swiss miniature from 1484. Town Library, Berne.

157. The Battle of Granson. Swiss miniature from 1515. Burgundian cavalry in armour attacking Swiss infantry. 1476. Kantonbibliotek, Aarau.

158. Depreciating coinage at the Mint, 1337.
From a Swiss chronicle, 1484. Town Library, Berne.

9. View of Venice, from *Theatrum urbium,* by Braunius. 1572.

160. Ca d'Oro. Venetian palace. 1420–34.

161. The City Hall (Palazzo Vecchio), Florence. 1298–1314.

. Northern part of the wall round Avila, north-west of Madrid. Twelfth century.

4. Rue des marchands. Colmar, Alsace. Half-timbered houses from. *c.* 1600.

5. Quai du Rosaire, Bruges. The town's belfry is in the background. Thirteenth to fourteenth century.

166. Hanseatic kogge (a sailing
ship peculiar to the Hanseatic
towns of the Middle Ages). The
seal of the town of Elbing. 1350.

167 a and b. Bridge over the Seine
showing traffic and merchants.
French miniature from
La Légende de St Denis. 1317.
Bibliothèque de l'Arsenal.

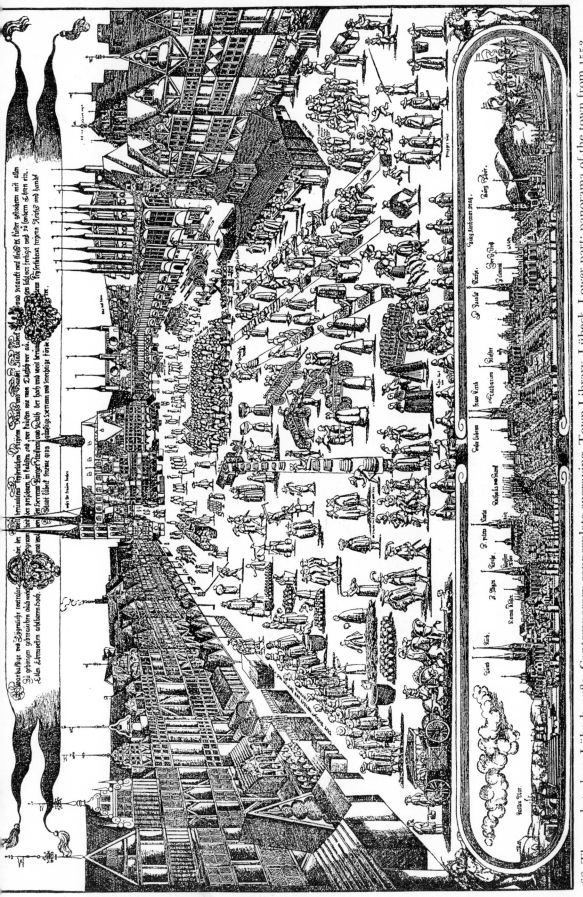

168. The market place, Lübeck, 1580. Contemporary copperplate engraving. Town Library, Lübeck. Lower part: panorama of the town from 1552.

169. Shops and traders. French miniature from *Les Éthiques d'Aristote*. Fifteenth century. Library in Rouen.

o. Noah's ark. Carpenters at work. From *The Bedford Hours*. Fourteenth century. British Museum.

171. Sword-maker and cutler. German sketch. *c.* 1500.

172. Building scene. The founding of Rome. From the Livius Manuscript in the Bibliothèque de l'Arsenal. *c.* 1465. (King Louis XI in the foreground.)

3. Visit to the doctor. Flemish
miniature from *Des Propriétéz
s Choses*. Late fifteenth century.
itish Museum.

174. Washing scene. From
Splendor Solis. 1582.
British Museum.

5. A baker is punished for having sold underweight bread. From *The Decretals of Gregory IX*.
1400. British Museum.

176. The Trinity blesses the married couple. From the *Traités divers*, by Jean Mansel. *c.* 1490. Bibliothèque de l'Arsenal.

177. School for the sons of distinguished noblemen. Fifteenth century. British Museum.

178. Agricultural workers. Flemish miniature. Early sixteenth century. British Museum.

179. Corn harvest. From *Les très riches heures du Duc de Berry. c.* 1415. Musée Condé, Chantilly.

. Different kinds of amusement: a game played on a board, a
l-game, and playing a recorder and stringed instruments. Minia-
e. Fifteenth century. British Museum.

181. Satirizing the tournament. The Luttrell Psalter. *c.* 1340. British Museum.

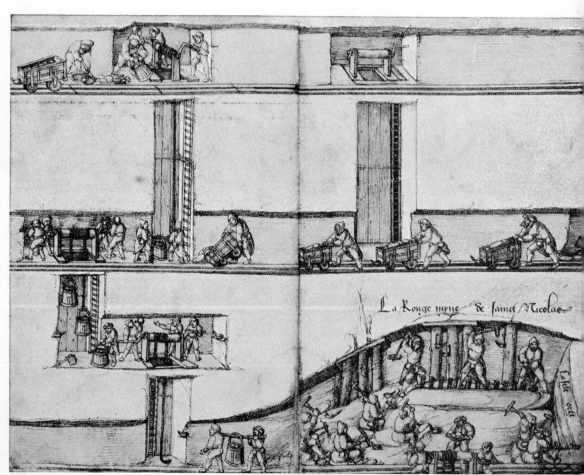

La Rouge myne de sainct Nicolae

182. Mining. Work in the shafts and galleries at the St Nicholas mine in Lorraine. Sketch by H. Gro[s]
Early sixteenth century. Bibliothèque de l'Ecole des Beaux-Arts, Paris.

. Winter scene from *Breviarium Grimani*. Flemish miniature. *c.* 1500. The Library of St Mark,
ice.

184. Ratha. Relief from the
Temple of Vishnu, Deogarh,
India. The wise men praise
Brahma. *c.* 500 A.D.

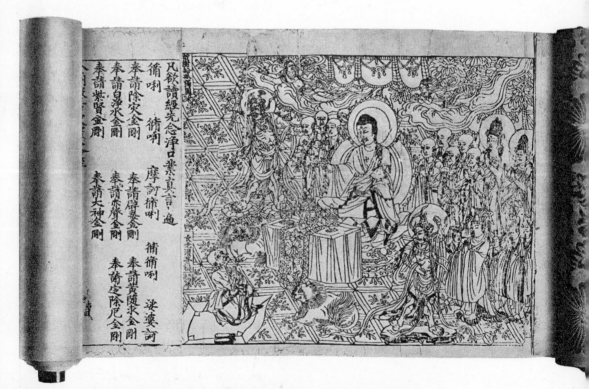

185. The oldest printed book in the world. Chinese, 868. British Museum.

. The Angkor-Vat Temple. Cambodia.
elfth century A.D.

187. The oldest known picture of printing.
Paris, 1507.

188. The Great Wall of China. The world's largest building operation – 2500 km. long, 8 m. high, and 5 to 8 m. wide. Erected in the third century B.C., but rebuilt and extended in the period 1350 to 1650 A.D.

189. The Temple of the Imperial Ancestors. Wooden building. Peking. Probably seventeenth centur

90. Persian miniature. Baysunqur's Shahnameh. Gulnare sees Ardashir, founder of the Sassanid Dynasty, from a window and falls in love with him. *c.* 1430.

191. Reconstruction of Christopher Columbus' caravel *Niña*.

192. Spanish cardinal baptizing
Moors after the fall of Granada,
1492. Relief by Philip de Borgoña
in the Capella Real (Chapel
Royal), Granada. *c.* 1520.

193. Aztec king surrenders to Cortés. Indian drawing. *c.* 1550.

. Transport of military supplies for the Cortés campaign to recapture Tenochtitlán, Mexico, in 1521.
lian drawing. *c.* 1550.

195. The Sun Pyramid at San Juan de Teotihuacán, Mexico. Length of side, 200 m. Height, approximately 65 m. Seventh to tenth century A.D.

196. Terrace cultivation in the days of the Incas in the Urumba Valley near Pisae, Peru.

7. Fuggerei, Augsburg. The oldest large-scale social-welfare buildings (106 dwellings) in Germany. ected in 1519 by Jacob Fugger II. In the foreground is a fountain dated 1595.

8. Pilgrimage to the wonder-working image of Mary at Regensburg. Section of an engraving by Ostendorffer. 1519.

199. Bad Hornhausen, 1646. Section of an engraving from Merian's *Theatrum europaeum V*, 1647.

o. The Emperor Maximilian attends Mass in Augsburg. Wood engraving by Petrarcameister. *c.* 1518.

201. Charles V enters Bruges, 1515. Contemporary Flemish miniature.

2. The Last Supper, by Leonardo da Vinci. Wall painting in Santa Maria delle Grazie, Milan. *c.* 1495.

203. The School of Athens, by Raphael. Stanza della Segnatura in the Vatican. 1508–24.

204. The creation of Adam, by Michelangelo. Ceiling painting in the Sistine Chapel, Vatican. 1508-12.

205. The Church of St Peter and St Peter's Square. The church was built by various architects from 1 onward. The square was laid out by Bernini, 1656–67 (see groundplan No. 20).

206. Luther as an Augustinian friar,
by Lucas Cranach the Elder.
Engraving. 1520.

207. Jean Calvin.
Ascribed to Holbein the Younger.
The Museum, Epinal.

208. Tomb of noble lady (Valentine Birague), by Germain Pilon. 1572. Louvre.

209. The Chateau of Chambord (Loire-et-Cher). Seen from the north. Built by Francis I, 1519 onward (see groundplan No. 21).

. The Ambassadors (Jean de Dinteville and Georges de Selve), by Holbein the Younger. 1533.
tional Gallery, London.

211. Protestant service. Part of a wood engraving by Lucas Cranach the Younger. After 1547.

2. The assassination of Henri IV of France in 1610 and Ravaillac's punishment. Contemporary
rman engraving.

213. Henri IV. Detail of a painting by Jacques Bunel. 1590–93. Private collection.

214. Henry VIII. Detail of cartoon for a mural in
Whitehall by Holbein the Younger. 1537.
National Portrait Gallery, London.

215. Henry VIII in his later years,
by an unknown artist.
National Portrait Gallery, London.

216. Queen Elizabeth I.
The Ditchley portrait. By an unknown
artist as a memorial of the queen's
visit to Ditchley, September 20, 1592.
National Portrait Gallery, London.

7. The Spanish Armada battles with the English fleet in the Channel, as depicted in a Gobelin
pestry made in the time of James I. The Gobelin tapestries hung in the old House of Lords, but they
re destroyed in the fire of 1834. This is an engraving from one of them.

218. The execution of Mary,
Queen of Scots, February 8, 1587.
Pen sketch by Elizabeth's secretary,
Robert Beale, who read the
sentence before the execution.
British Museum.

219. Philip II of Spain with his son and three of his four queens at prayer,
by Pompeio Leoni. In the chancel at the Escorial. c. 1595.

Malines (Mechelen) plundered by the Spaniards, October 1, 1572. Contemporary engraving by ns Hogenberg, who was born there.

221. Surrender of Breda, 1625, by Velasquez. 1635. The Prado Museum, Madrid.

MOSCOVIA VRBS METROPOLIS TO:
tius Rufsiæ Albæ.

2. Prospect of Moscow in the sixteenth century. The Kremlin and the Cathedral of St Basil in the
ntre. From Braunius's *Theatrum urbium.*

223. The Cathedral of St Basil in Moscow. Built 1554–60 by the architects Barma and Postnik for Ivan the Terrible to commemorate the conquest of Kazan. Restored 1954.

224. Palm Sunday procession on the square in front of the Kremlin, now Red Square. To the left is St Basil's. Engraving by Rotgiesser in Olearius's *Travels*. 1647.

R.Holata Outina.

225. Ceremonies by North
American Indians after a
victory. Print by de Bry, 1590,
engraving from a watercolour
by John White, 1587.

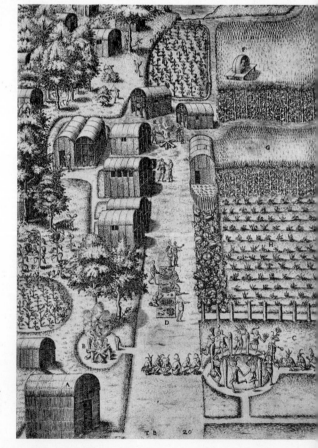

226. Indian village of
Secota in Virginia. Print by
de Bry. 1590.

a. The Turks before Vienna, 1529. View of the Turkish camp. Drawing by Bartholomäus Beham.

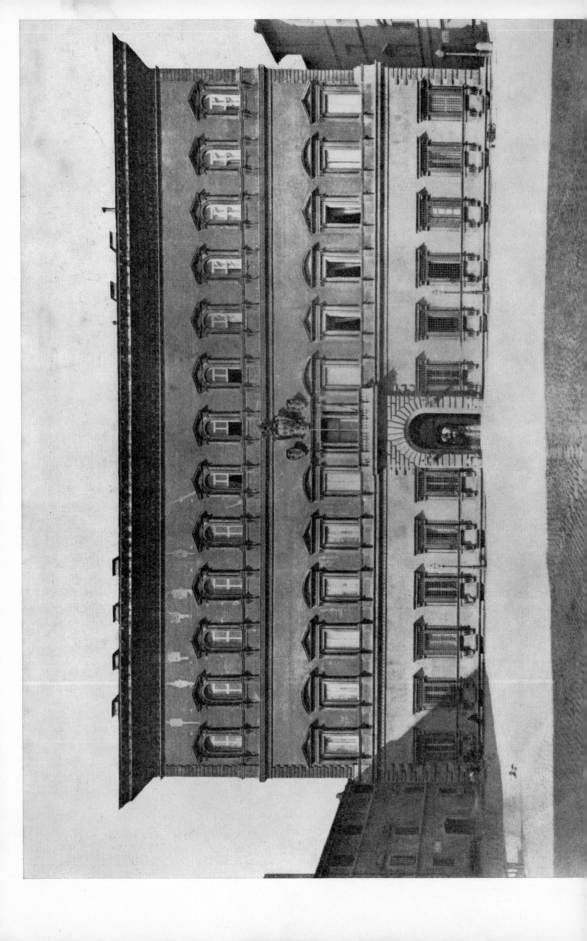

227 c. Lukas von Hildebrandt's Belvedere in Vienna which he built for Prince Eugene of Savoy between 1714 and 1723.

228. Richelieu, by Claude Mellan. *c.* 1640.
National Museum, Stockholm.

229. (a) Musketeer and (b) pikeman. Prints by Jacques de Gheyn. 1608.

. Queen Anne of Austria and the Dauphin visit a hospital in Paris, by A. Bosse. Musée Carnavalet.

. Winter interior. Preparations for Shrove Tuesday, by A. Bosse. Print. *c.* 1635.

232. Louis XIV, 1665. Detail of a painting by
Philippe de Champaigne, in the Museum in
Grenoble.

233. Detail of No. 234.

4. Louis XIV in coronation robes, 1701, by Hyacinthe Rigaud. (2.79 m. x 1.90 m.) Louvre.

235. Louis XIV and Colbert visit the Gobelin factory, by Le Brun. Gobelin tapestry.

236. The Hall of Venus, with a statue of Louis XIV by Warin. An apartment at Versailles.

237. Versailles. The palace was built by Le Vau and Jules Hardouin Mansart and completed in 1682. The gardens were laid out by Le Nôtre.

238. Syndics of the cloth guild, by Rembrandt. 1662. Rijksmuseum, Amsterdam.

239. The Feast of St Nicholas, by Jan Steen. c. 1665. Rijksmuseum, Amsterdam.

Children's games, by P. Brueghel the Elder. 1560. Detail of a painting in the Kunsthistorisches
seum, Vienna.

241. Scenes from the manufacture of porcelain. Chinese sketch, coloured. Eighteenth century.

DIT HVYS IS TE HVER

THIS HOVSE IS TO LETT

Be gone you rogues you have sate long enough

C. Capel.   C. Law.   G. O. Cromwel.   This is an Oule.

. Cromwell dissolves Parliament, April 20, 1653. Contemporary satirical broadsheet (Dutch).

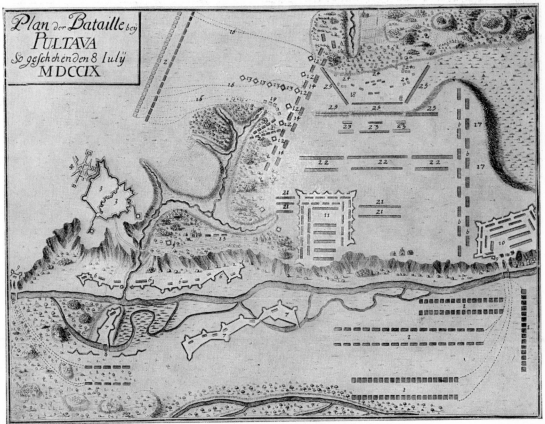

Plan der Bataille bey PULTAVA So geschehen den 8 Iulÿ MDCCIX

243. Plan of the Battle of Poltava, July 8, 1709. From Matthæus Merian's *Theatrum europaeum*.

244. Autumn pastoral. Detail of a painting by Boucher. 1749. Wallace Collection, London.

245. Peasant family at mealtime, by Louis Le Nain. c. 1642. Louvre.

. "It's a boy!" by J. M. Moreau the Younger. Print from *Histoire des Modes et du Costume*. 1777.

247. L'Enseigne de Gersaint (Gersaint's shop-sign), by Antoine Watteau. 1720. Dahlem Museum, Berlin.

. Wig-maker and barber. *La Grande Encyclopédie,* Book VIII.

249. Frederick the Great, by Anton Graff. 1781. Sans Souci, Potsdam

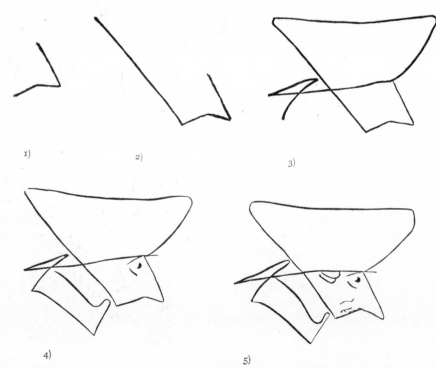

1)

2)

3)

4)

5)

250. Caricature of Frederick the Great, by W. Busch (drawn in one continuous line). *c.* 1860.

Russian prisoners in Berlin, 1758. Etching by Chodowiecki.

The king's cake, by B. N. Lemire. Contemporary political allegory on the first partition of
nd, 1772, showing Catherine the Great of Russia, Stanislas II of Poland, Joseph II of Austria,
Frederick the Great of Prussia.

253. Illustrations by Chodowiecki in Basedow's *Elementarwerke,* 1774, showing various punishmer and various crafts.

254. Peasants destroy a balloon (Montgolfier's) which fell in the village of Gonesse, 1783. Contempo anonymous copperplate print.

The Worsley-Manchester Canal, 1770. The entrance to the underground canal tunnel
n the coalfields at Worsley.

Bathing machines, by Thomas Rowlandson, from Henry Wigstead and Thomas Rowlandson:
Excursion to Brighthelmstone (Brighton) *made in the year 1789*. 1790.

257. Members of a women's society in North Carolina vow not to drink tea until their country is free. Anonymous engraving. 1774.

258. Electioneering – Canvassing for votes – by William Hogarth. 1757. Soane Museum, London.

259 a. The American Declaration of Independence, July 4, 1776, by John Trumbull. 1790. Yale University, U. S. A.

259 c. Holkham Hall, Norfolk, the south side of the central block (1734). Architects, William Kent and Matthew Brettingham (see groundplan No. 23).

260. The Chinese Room at Schönbrunn, Vienna. *c.* 1750.

. Pavilion at a corner of the Zwinger Palace, Dresden. Built by M. Pöppelmann, 1711–22. Sculptured
:orations by B. Permoser, for August II.

262. The dying Marat, by J. L. David. (1.65 m. x 1.28 m.). 1793. Musée Royal des Beaux-Arts, Brusse

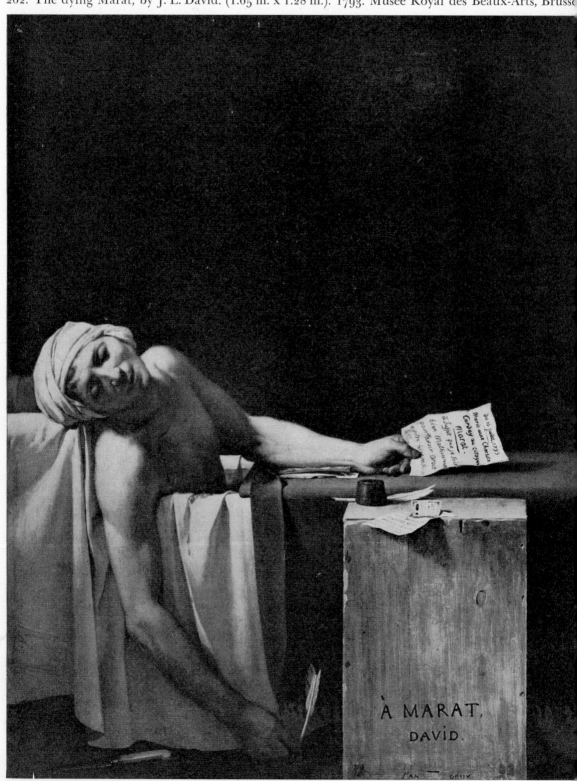

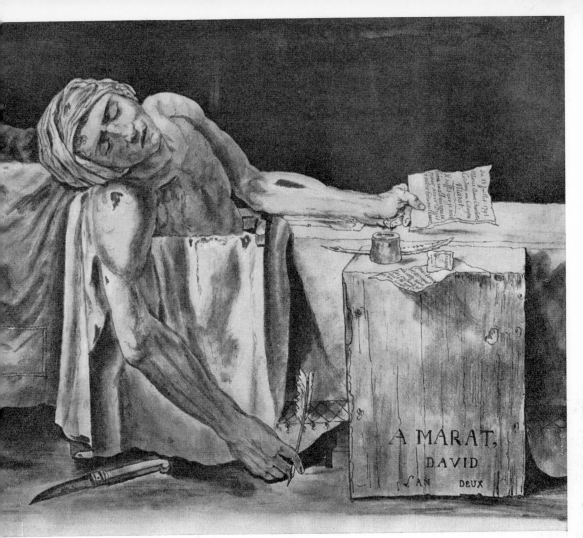

Sketch for "The dying Marat," possibly by J. L. David. 1793.

264. Marie Antoinette with her children, by Elisabeth-Louise Vigée-Lebrun. 1788. National Museu
Versailles.

265. Sketch of "Widow Capet" in the tumbrel on the way to the guillotine, October 16 1793, by J. L. David. Louvre.

266. A woman of the people. Attributed to J. L. David. 1794. Musée des Beaux-Arts, Lyon.

. Madame de Laporte, a noblewoman, by J. M. Nattier. 1752. National Gallery of Art, Washington.

268. Sketch of Danton,
by J. L. David. 1794. Lille.

269. Georges Jacques Danton, possibly by J. L. David. Musée Carnavalet, Paris.

. The wounded Robespierre, who was placed on a table in the hall outside the room of the Com-
ttee of Public Safety at the Tuileries after his arrest. He was guillotined on the following day,
y 28, 1794 (10th Thermidor, Year II). Engraving by Duplessi-Bertaux.

271. Rebels bring the head of the murdered Ferraud, a member of the Convention, to the rostrum the Convention Chamber, May 20, 1795 (1st Prairial, Year III). Engraving by Duplessi-Bertaux.

General Bonaparte, by J. L. David. Uncompleted
ating. *c.* 1797. Louvre.

273. Napoleon at St Cloud, 1812. Drawn from life by A. S. Girodet.
Musée de Châteauroux.

275. Horatio, Viscount Nelson,
by L. F. Abbott. *c.* 1797.
National Portrait Gallery, London.

. Imaginary representation of French plans for the invasion of England. Anonymous print. 1804.

277. "The Spanish bull fight or the Corsican matador in danger," by J. Gillray. Contemporary satiri[c]
print relating to Napoleon's campaign in Spain. 1808.

278. Crossing the Beresina, 1812, by Albrecht Adam. During his disastrous retreat from Moscow
Napoleon crossed this river with the remnant – 12,000 men – of his invading army of 600,000.

. Congress of Vienna, 1815. Engraving by Godefroy, 1819, from the painting by J. B. Isabey, 1814–15.

. A game of draughts in the Café Lamblin, by L. L. Boilly. *c.* 1820. Musée Condé, Chantilly.

281. Liberty leads the people, by Eugène Delacroix. The Revolution of July 28, 1830. 1831. (2.60 m. x 3.25 m.). Louvre.

The Franco-English *rapprochement*, 1844. Queen Victoria receives Louis Philippe in the drawing-
m car of her special train. Engraving
n the contemporary watercolour by
gret.

283. How deep one sinks! by Honoré Daumier. The
urchins of Paris in the Tuileries. February 1848.

285. Napoleon III. Photograph.
c. 1860.

284. Napoleon III, by Hippolyte Flandrin.
1863. National Museum, Versailles.

286. Electoral reform in England. Cartoon by John Doyle, November 1831. John Bull is indignant, pulling Lord Grey, who pulls after him the resisting King William IV.

The Capitol. The Congress building in Washington, D.C., 1827. Built 1793–1800.

The Houses of Parliament, London. Built 1840–65, from the designs of Charles Barry and
V. N. Pugin.

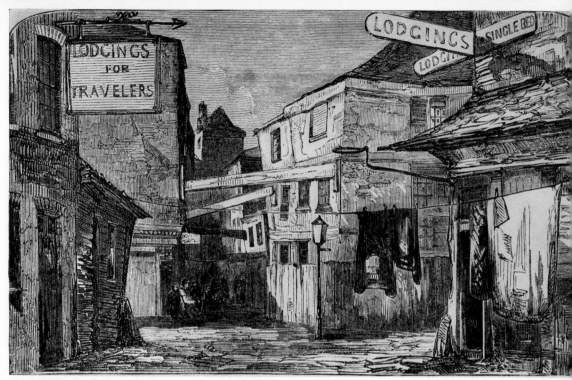

289. London slums. Duke Street, Southwark. 1851.

290. Rebuilt area after slum clearance. Swedenborg Square, Stepney, London. *c.* 1920.

291. Young girl pulling coal-tub in sixteen- to twenty-two-inch-high gallery in coal-mine. 1842.

. Satirical drawing by George Cruikshank, directed against women delighted with the cheapness of hing. c. 1840.

293. A steam-driven "coach," constructed in 1859 by Thomas Rickett.

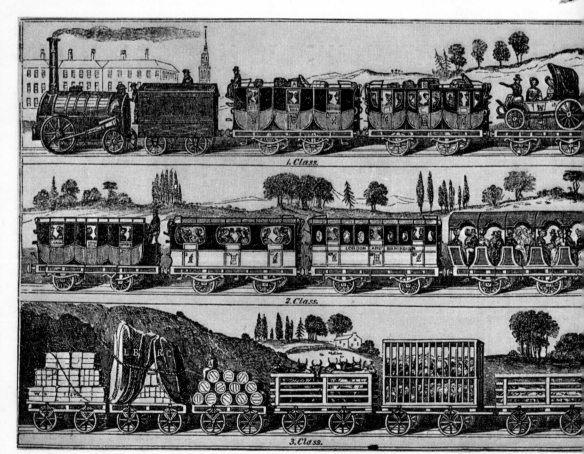

294. The London-to-Birmingham railway, opened 1833. This 1837 print shows the rolling-stock.

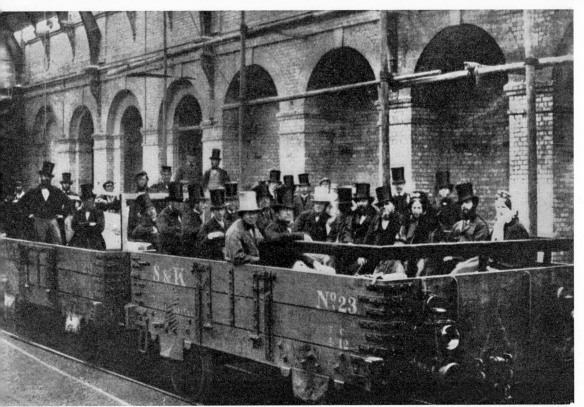

5. The London underground railway, opened January 9, 1863. To the left in the foremost carriage
Gladstone (?).

6. Robert Fulton's steamship, *Clermont,* on the way from New York to Albany via the Hudson River,
10. Lithograph by an unknown artist.

297. River with boats, by Hiroshige, Japanese, 1797–1858. Woodcut. Early nineteenth century.

8. Barricade outside Kölnisches Rathaus in Berlin, March 18–19, 1848. Woodcut from *Leipzig ustrierte Zeitung*, April 15, 1848 (see groundplan No. 24).

299. Wrangel's new street-sweeping machine in action in Berlin in March 1848. Cartoon by Kaspar Braun in *Fliegende Blätter,* 1848.

300. Karl Marx.

301. Crimean War. British sappers in a captured flank position at Sebastopol look for an electric cable probably connected with the powder magazine. Photograph by Fenton. 1855.

302. Victor Emmanuel, Cavour, and Garibaldi. *c.* 1859.

303. Proclamation of the German Empire at Versailles, January 18, 1871. Drawing in *Leipzig Illustr Zeitung*, 1871.

304. Proclamation at Versailles, January 18, 1871, by A. von Werner. Painted in 1885 for the "Herrscherhalle" in the Arsenal, Berlin.

The advantages and disadvantages of crinolines. Section of a German lithograph (in colour).
eteenth century.

306. The triumph of the Communes.
Contemporary satirical drawing by F. Mathis.

307. Iron sheet-rolling works at Königshütte, Upper Silesia, by Adolph Menzel. Painted, 1875.

8. Closing session of the Berlin Congress, Berlin City Hall, by A. von Werner. Painted, 1878–81.

9. Police dissolve a workers' meeting in Berlin, 1890. *Leipzig Illustrierte Zeitung*, 1890.

310. W. E. Gladstone,
by John E. Millais. 1879.
National Portrait Gallery,
London.

311. Caricatures of
Gladstone.
Punch, 1891.

"an Old Woman"

an old
schoolmaster

"a Caricature"

312. Otto von Bismarck,
by Franz von Lenbach.
c. 1885. Owned by the Pope.

313. Caricature of Lenbach and his numerous
Bismarck pictures, by F. A. von Kaulbach,
in the Munich paper *Allotria*, 1883.

314. The meeting of Livingstone and Stanley in Ujiji, November 10, 1871. Contemporary woodcut.

"NEW CROWNS FOR OLD ONES!"

315. "New crowns for old ones!"
Disraeli presents Queen Victoria with
her crown as Empress of India.
Punch, April 15, 1876.

German troops suppress a revolt in German East Africa. *Leipzig Illustrierte Zeitung*, 1888.

317. General Robert Baden-Powell enters Pretoria, May 1900. Drawing by Melton Prior. *Illustrated London News*, 1900.

318. Lieutenant Binger rides into Kong on the Ivory Coast and claims the country between the Upper Niger and the coast as a French Protectorate, 1880. Contemporary watercolour by Tinayre. Musée de la France d'Outre-Mer, Paris.

319. Abraham Lincoln meets General McClellan at a camp in Maryland during the American Civil War in 1862. Photograph.

Cotton harvest in the U.S.A. early in the nineteenth century. Contemporary woodcut.

. Indians attack immigrants crossing the prairie. Painted in Düsseldorf by Charles Wimar (1828–62)
m a report by a French eyewitness. University of Michigan Museum of Arts.

322. Alexander Graham Bell demonstrates the first telephone in Philadelphia, February 14, 187
Contemporary woodcut.

323. Port Arthur's last nights, 1905. Japanese military observers watch fr a balloon the effect of the bombardment on the town, the harbour, and the defences. *L'Illustration*, January 7, 1905.

. "Bloody Sunday." Russian cavalry charge the crowd in St Petersburg, January 22, 1905. *L'Illustra- n*, January 28, 1905. Drawing from a sketch made by its special correspondent.

325. The charm of tennis. "She: 'Yours or mine, Sir Charles?' He: 'Yours, awfully yours.'" Drawing George du Maurier. *Punch*, October 13, 1883.

326. A cycle club in the Bois de Boulogne, Paris, by Jean Beraud. *c.* 1900. Musée des Sceaux.

. Ellehammer's helicopter-like two-decker flying-machine in which he was the first in Europe to get the earth in a motor-driven aeroplane. September 12, 1906.

328. Henry Ford and his wife in the first Ford, made in 1896. Later photograph.

329. Auvers, by Vincent van Gogh. 1890.

0. German submarine in action against a British ship. *Leipzig Illustrierte Zeitung*, 1915.

. The first tank, used in the Battle of the Somme, September 15, 1916. *L'Illustration*, 1916.

332. British statesmen of World War I, by James Guthrie. 1921–30. National Portrait Gallery, Lond
(Among others, Lloyd George, Churchill, Grey, Balfour, and Asquith.)

333. French trench, 1917. Awaiting a gas attack.

334. German generals in World War I. From the left: Ludendorff, Hindenburg, and Hoffma
Leipzig Illustrierte Zeitung, 1914.

5. Clemenceau speaks in the Chamber of Deputies on Armistice Day, November 11, 1918.
Illustration, 1918.

6. The Big Four at Versailles, March 25, 1919. Lloyd George, Orlando, Clemenceau, and Wilson.

337. Lenin speaks to the people, 1917.

338. Lenin surrounded by representatives of the workers at the second All-Russia Congress, 1921.

. Hitler speaks at a meeting of the German Labour Party, October 19, 1919, by H. V. Hoyer. This
~~ture~~ was painted at a later date, but it has been proved to be accurate.

. Locarno Conference, October 5, 1925. From the left: Stresemann, Austen Chamberlain, and Briand.

341. Mustapha Kemal Atatür
checks the knowledge of
officials of the Latin alphabe
The Latin alphabet became
compulsory in Turkey in 19

342. Stresemann speaks at the delegate meeting of the League of Nations on Germany's entry.
September 10, 1926.

The first radio transmission in London, February 23, 1921, with the singer Lauritz Melchior at microphone.

The first public demonstration of television in the U.S.A., April 7, 1927.

345. Mussolini in 1928.

346. Mussolini in 1944. His regime came to
an end on July 25, 1943, following the
invasion of S

Wall Street collapses on October 23, 1929 – "Black Thursday." The crowd outside the Stock hange and the large banks in New York.

Guernica, by Pablo Picasso (1937). The town of Guernica in Northern Spain was destroyed by ematic bombing by German planes on April 26, 1937, during the Spanish Civil War. Museum of dern Art, New York.

349. Adolf Hitler.

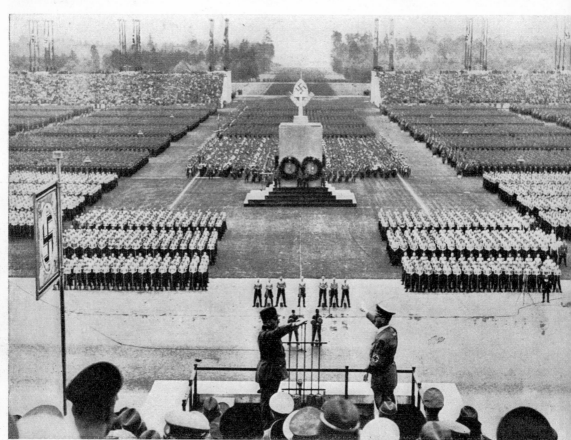

350. Nazi demonstration. Hitler holds a parade of 40,000 workers. 1938.

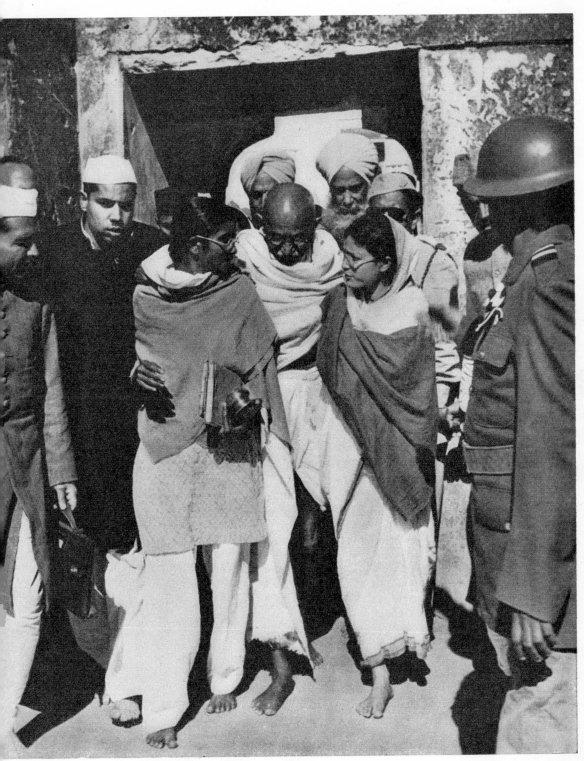

1. Mahatma Gandhi with disciples. *c.* 1945.

352. Conference in Munich, September 29, 1938. From the left: Goering, Hitler, Ciano, Mussolini, Daladier, and Neville Chamberlain.

353. German troops move into Czechoslovakia, March 15, 1939.

4. Concluding the German-Russian Agreement, August 24, 1939, in Moscow. From the left: Ribben-
•p, Secretary-of-State Gaus, Stalin, and Molotov.

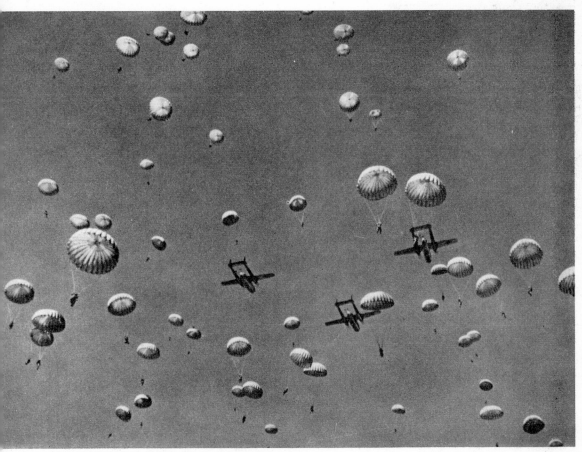

5. American airborne troops dropped by parachute.

356. Winston Churchill in
his siren suit, 1943.

357. Morale in
Britain during the
blitz of 1940.
According to German
statements the
British were panic-
stricken. *Punch*,
August 14, 1940.

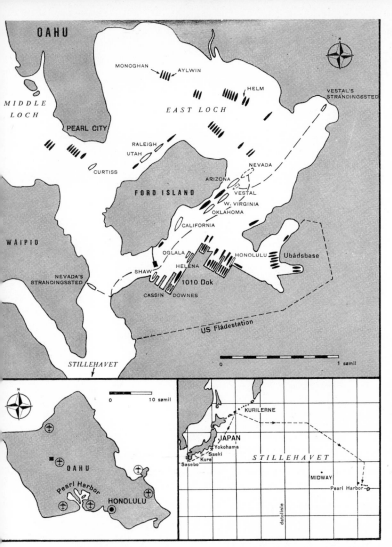

358. Situation plan of Pearl Harbor, December 7, 1941. The blank ship symbols indicate ships that were sunk or seriously damaged. The map below to the right shows the route of the Japanese to Pearl Harbor.

359. The attack on Pearl Harbor, December 7, 1941. The battleship *Oklahoma* has been sunk, *West Virginia* is badly damaged. Five battleships, five destroyers, and one minelayer were sunk. Three battleships, three destroyers, and several smaller craft were damaged.

360. The Battle of Stalingrad (now Volgograd). Russian troops move out through the shattered stree
The German troops surrendered on January 31, 1943.

361. Teheran Conference, November 28 to December 1, 1943. Sitting: Stalin, Roose-
velt, Churchill. Standing: Hopkins, Molotov, Harriman, Clark Kerr, Eden.

2. Invasion of Normandy, June 6, 1944 (D-day). Mulberry B Harbour. Blockships and Phoenix
ssons act as a breakwater, the importance of which is clear from the picture.

3. Invasion of Normandy. D-day. Barrage balloons protect the ships and transports against surprise
ack by enemy planes.

364. Hitler's headquarters after the attempted assassination, July 20, 1944. The arrow marks where the bomb was placed.

365. V-I flying-bomb falling on London, 1944.

. The Stars and Stripes placed on the mountain top, Suribachi, Iwo Jima, February 19, 1945.

367. Representatives of the German Wehrmacht meet Field-Marshal Montgomery in his tent on Lüneburg Heath for the capitulation conditions. May 4, 1945.

368. The concentration camp at Belsen, 1945. Many of the prisoners lived only a short time after their release.

9. The atom bomb explodes over Nagasaki, August 9, 1945.

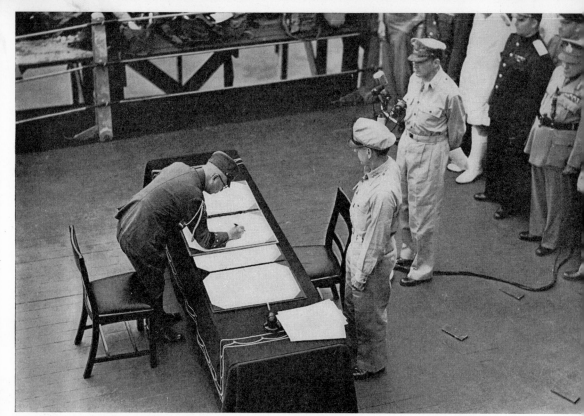

370. Japan's unconditional surrender on board the battleship *Missouri*, September 2, 1945. Gene... MacArthur is at the microphones.

371. The Emperor Hirohito abandons the tradition of the dynasty's divine origins when Japan adopts a democratic constitution.

Russian caricature during the war. Karl Marx's doctrine
understood by the reformer Kautsky.

373. Russian dam for a power-station on the River Ural.

374. The State University on the Lenin Hills, west of Moscow. Built 1948–53.

375. The Unité d'Habitation at Marseilles, built by Le Corbusier, 1946–52.

376. Homeless refugees in
Hongkong. The boy lives
in the basket against which
he is leaning.

. Pipelines through rugged country to the refineries in Abadan, which are probably the largest in
world. *Illustrated London News,* January 4, 1947.

378. British troops leave Egypt. *Illustrated London News,* 1946.

379. Farming on a kibbutz, a voluntarily established collective farm of Israel. The workers are using turia – a special weeding-hoe.

ɔ. Former Secretary-of-State of the U.S.A., Dean Acheson, gives an account of the development of NATO in Lisbon, 1952. The map shows the NATO countries at that time.

381. Communist soldiers entering Peking, 1949.

382. China's first tractor factory begins production. Eight different types of tractor are made to me the requirements of the different farming terrain.

383. The Chairman of the Chinese Communist Party of the Chinese People's Republic, Mao Tse-Tu holds a meeting – with tea-drinking – of the Supreme Council, 1959. Facing him is Vice-Chairman the People's Government Council Soong Ching Lin (sister of Madame Chiang Kai-Shek) and Panchen Lama from Tibet.

4. United Nations headquarters, Manhattan, New York, seen from the East River. The 38-storey
ilding houses the Secretariat. The low building in front holds, among other things, the Security
uncil's meeting-place.

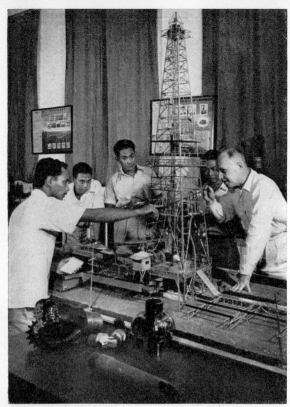

385. Indonesian technicians study the layout of an oil-boring tower under the guidance of a Dutch instructor. 1955.

386. The Bhakra Dam in India. More than 12,000 workers were employed here (1960).

1. President de Gaulle in Mostaganem, Algiers, May 7, 1958. The Mohammedans flock around him.

392. The Russian cosmonaut
Major Yuri Gagarin in his
spacesuit. He was the first man to
travel round the world in space.
November 7, 1961.

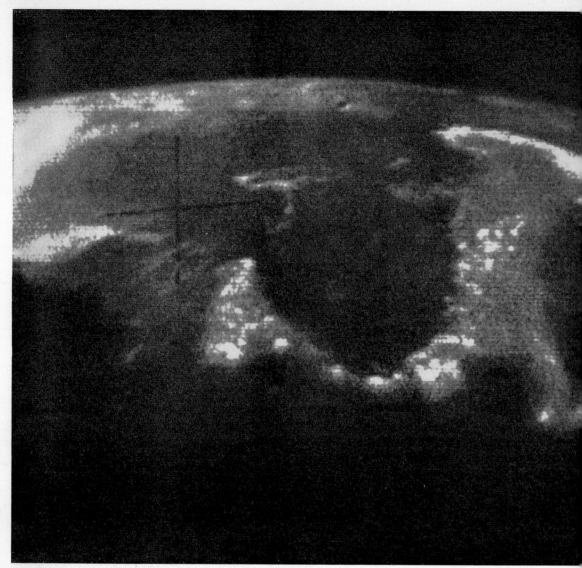

393. The earth (Italy) seen from the American satellite *Tiros I*. 1960.

394. A space rocket takes the air, shot from its underground launching-chamber at Cape Canaveral (now Cape Kennedy). November 17, 1961.

. East German guards (Vopos) use a mirror to try to discourage observers on the West Berlin side he wall, which, since August 13, 1961, has separated East Berlin from West Berlin. 1962.

. One of the last duties of Dag Hammarskjöld, as Secretary-General of the United Nations from 1953 September 17, 1961, was to meet the President of Katanga, Moise Tshombe. September 1961.

397. Chancellor Adenauer visits President and Mrs Kennedy at the White House, Washington, in 19

398. The American astronaut John Glenn (in spacesuit) studies his directions for flyin operations during training for the space journey which he carried out on February 2 1962.

President de Gaulle at the Joan-of-Arc celebrations in Orléans, 1959.

400. American aerial photograph which shows the Soviet launching-pads for offensive missiles under construction on Cuba. October 1962.

401. Indian women in the Home Guard being instructed in the use of the rifle. November 1962.

. Oak Ridge Atom Establishment, Tennessee, U. S. A. Established 1942.

. The early days of the production belt. The Ford Motor Company, 1913.

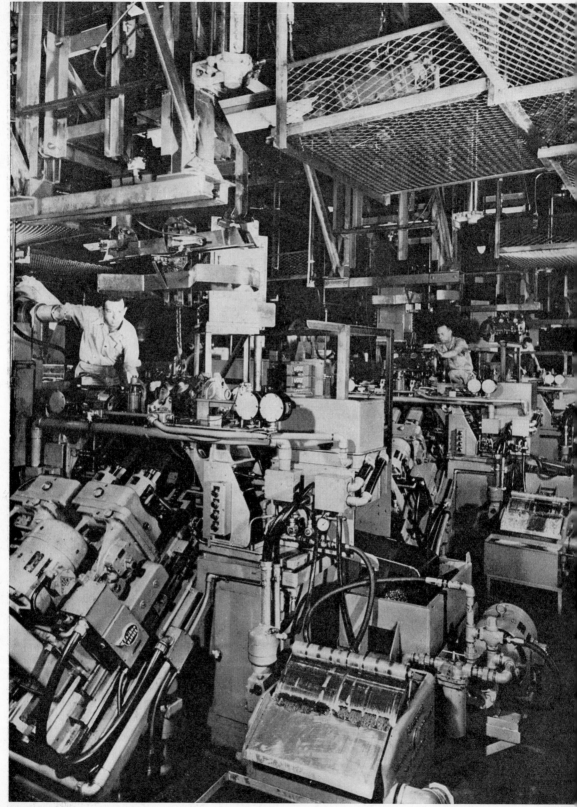

404. Fully automated factory. The Chevrolet factory, Flint, Michigan.

Country shop, by Hans Smidth. 1909. Statens Museum for Kunst, Copenhagen.

. Supermarket in New York, 1960.

407. Corn harvest on a Soviet collective farm.

408. Corn harvest on a farm in the Middle West, U.S.A.

409. Six-stream, one-way street in Sydney, Australia, at rush hour.

. Part of Coventry's newly built shopping centre. 1962.

411. Inside the ruins of Coventry Cathedral. The nave and chancel were destroyed in a German air
raid, November 14, 1940.

412. The interior of Coventry Cathedral in 1935 before its destruction.

. In the chancel of the ruined cathedral. The altar was made of stone from the ruins and the charred
s from badly burnt roof-beams.

. The new Coventry Cathedral seen from the east. Consecrated in May 1962. To the left are the
s of the former cathedral.

415. Eskimo family outside their home, Angmassalik. *c.* 1900.

416. Eskimo family in their home, East Greenland. 1960.

The Common Market Commission. From the left: Vice-President Jean Rey (Belgium), the Presi-
, Professor Hallstein (West Germany), and Vice-President Sicco Mansholt (Holland).

A reception after the Atom Conference in Moscow, August 5, 1963. Left to right: Adlai Stevenson,
n Rusk, Edward Heath, Gromyko, Khrushchev, and Sir Alec Douglas-Home (then the Earl of
ie).

419. President John F. Kennedy and Mrs Kennedy start their tour through Dallas on Friday, Noven 22, 1963.

420. A few seconds later, at 12.31, the President was hit in the head by an assassin's bullet. He collapsed, dying, and fell over towards Mrs Kennedy.

421. A section of the moon's surface on a map of the moon, drawn with the aid of powerful telescopes. The cross shows where the rocket Ranger 7 hit the moon, July 31, 1964.

422. Photograph of the moon's surface taken from Ranger 7 at a distance of 700 km. (see 421).

423. Chancellor Erhard and President Lyndon Johnson outside a church in Texas during the Chancellor's visit to America in 1964.

424. Brezhnev and Khrushchev during a meeting of the Supreme Soviet in Moscow. Behind them (to right): Grishin, Voronov, Polyansky, and Kirilenko.

25. An American helicopter landing in South Vietnam, 1967.

26. Race riots in Los Angeles, U.S.A., 1965.

427. The Prime Minister, Harold Wilson, in September 1966.

428. Egyptian soldiers taken prisoner by Israeli troops in the Sinai Desert in June 1967.

429. Television – a cultural problem. "We are terribly worried about William." *Punch,* 1954.

GROUNDPLANS

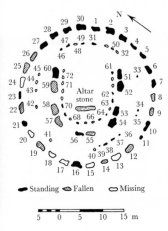

1. Plan of Stonehenge.

Standing Fallen Missing

5 0 5 10 15 m

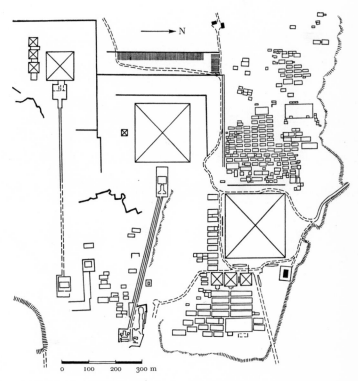

Plan of pyramids of Gizeh and graves.

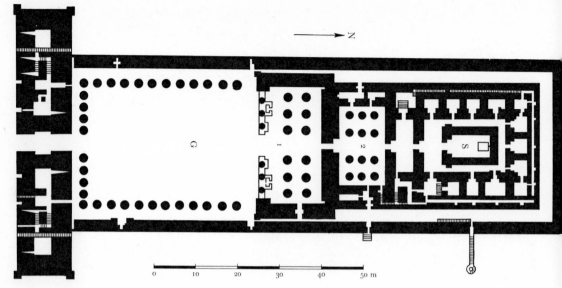

3. Plan of temple at Edfu.

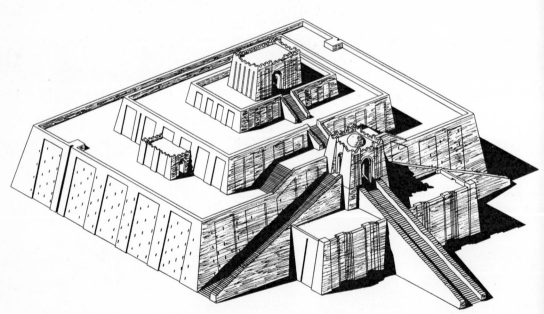

4. Reconstruction of Ziggurat (Ur).

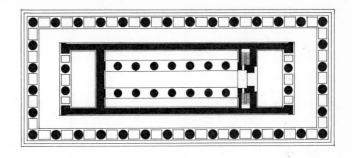

5. Plan of Greek temple (Paestum).

10   0   10   20   30 m

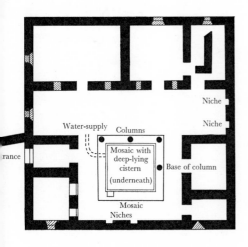

Niche

Niche

Water-supply   Columns

rance

Mosaic with
deep-lying
cistern
(underneath)   Base of column

Mosaic
Niches

6. Plan of Greek peristyle house at Delos. North side.

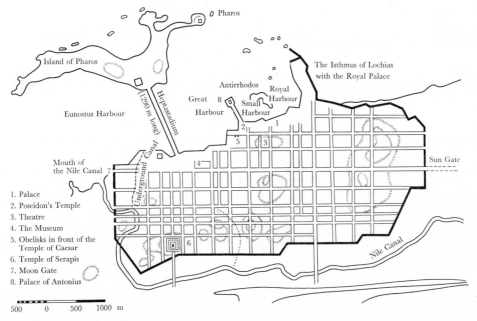

0 Pharos

Island of Pharos

The Isthmus of Lochias
with the Royal Palace

Antirrhodos   Royal
Harbour

Great   8
Harbour   Small
Harbour

Eunostus Harbour

(1290 m long)

Heptastadium

Underground Canal

Mouth of
the Nile Canal 7

Sun Gate

1. Palace
2. Poseidon's Temple
3. Theatre
4. The Museum
5. Obelisks in front of the
   Temple of Caesar
6. Temple of Serapis
7. Moon Gate
8. Palace of Antonius

Nile Canal

500   0   500   1000 m

7. Plan of ancient Alexandria.

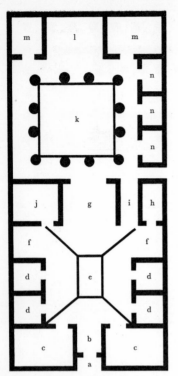

8 a. Plan of typical Roman house.

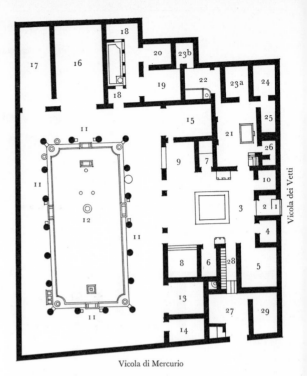

Vicola dei Vetti

Vicola di Mercurio

8 b. Plan of the house of the Vettii family. Pompeii.

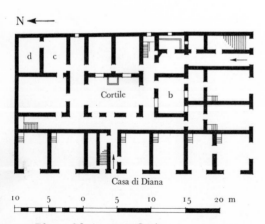

N ←

Cortile

Casa di Diana

10   5   0   5   10   15   20 m

9 a. Plan of houses at Ostia.

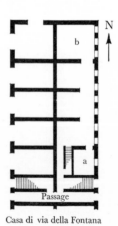

N ↑

Passage

Casa di via della Fontana

9 b. Reconstruction of the façade of Casa di Diana (see groundplan No. 9 a). Built *c.* 150 A.D.

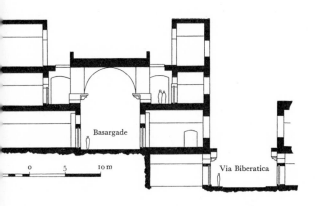

Basargade

Via Biberatica

0   5   10 m

10 a. Cross-section of Trajan's 'department store', seen from the north with the vaulted shopping street (*Basargade*) and the Via Biberatica.

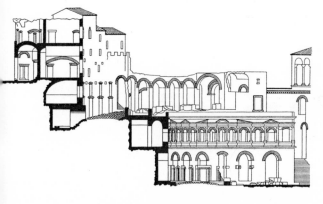

10 b. Cross-section through the middle of the 'store', showing the different terraces and the rock which the building rests on or penetrates.
Below to the right is the way to the forum in the middle of the Via Biberatica. Top left is a third street.

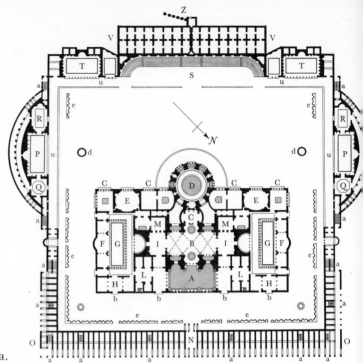

11. Plan of the Baths of Caracalla.

50　　　0　　　50　　　100 m

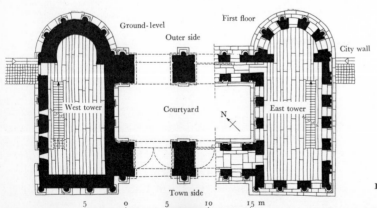

First floor

Ground-level

Outer side

City wall

West tower

Courtyard

N

East tower

Town side

5　　0　　5　　10　　15 m

12. Plan of Porta Nigra at Trier.

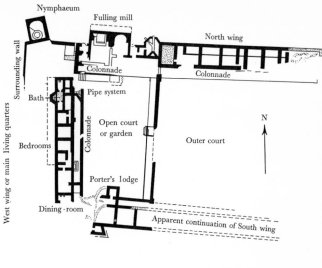

Nymphaeum

Fulling mill

North wing

Surrounding wall

Colonnade

Colonnade

Pipe system

Bath

N

West wing or main living quarters

Colonnade

Open court
or garden

Outer court

Bedrooms

Porter's lodge

Dining-room

Apparent continuation of South wing

13. Roman villa, Chedworth.

10   0   10   20   30   40   50 m

Ambo at which the Gospels were read

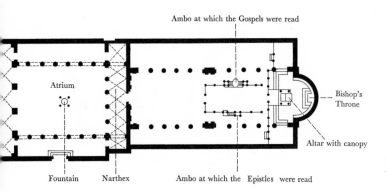

Atrium

Bishop's
Throne

Altar with canopy

Fountain   Narthex   Ambo at which the Epistles were read

14. Plan of early Christian
basilica San Clemente, Rome.

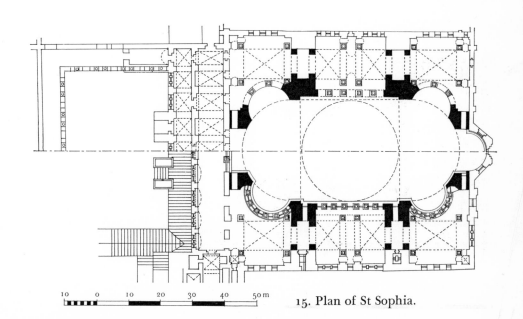

10   0   10   20   30   40   50 m

15. Plan of St Sophia.

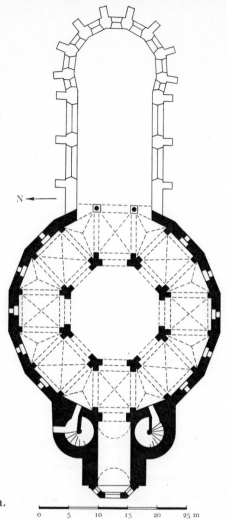

16. Plan of cathedral at Aachen.

N ←

0   5   10   15   20   25 m

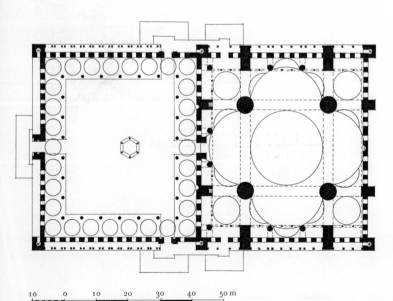

17. Plan of Mosque of Ahmed I i
Istanbul.

10   0   10   20   30   40   50 m

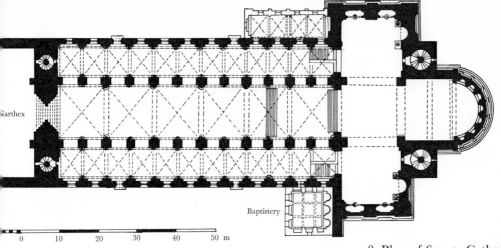

Narthex

Baptistery

0   10   20   30   40   50 m

18. Plan of Speyer Cathedral –
Romanesque.

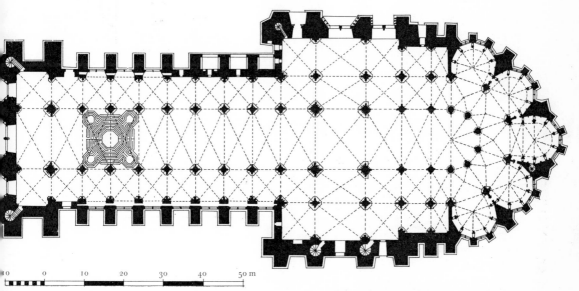

0   10   20   30   40   50 m

19. Plan of Reims Cathedral – Gothic.

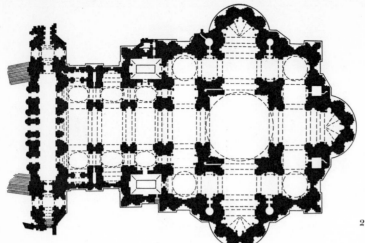

20. Plan of St. Peter's, Rome.

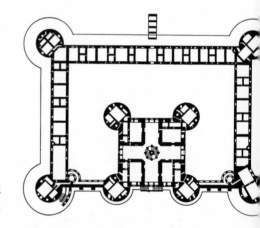

21. Plan of the Chateau de Chambord in the Loire Valley.

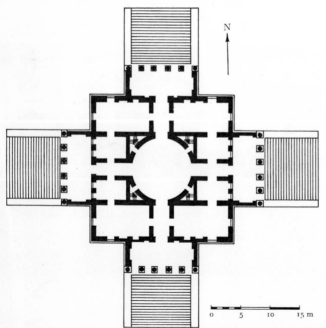

N

22. Palladio. Plan of Villa Rotonda.

0   5   10   15 m

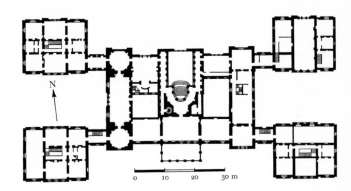

23. Plan of Holkham Hall, Norfolk.

0   10   20   30 m

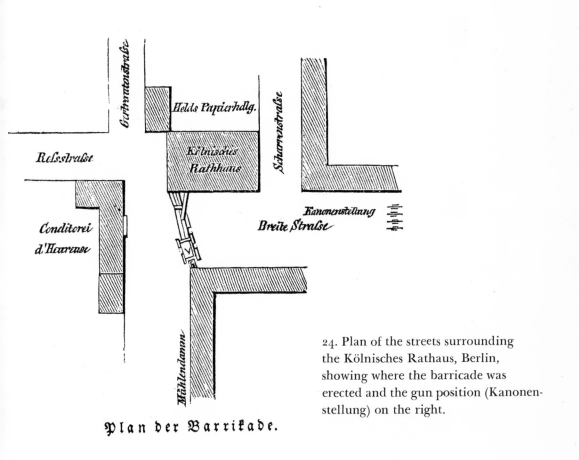

Plan der Barrikade.

24. Plan of the streets surrounding
the Kölnisches Rathaus, Berlin,
showing where the barricade was
erected and the gun position (Kanonen-
stellung) on the right.

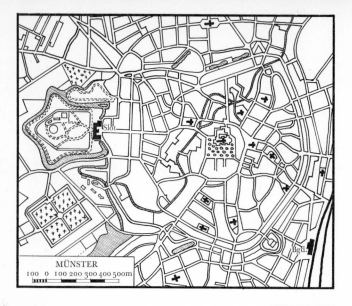

25. West German cathedral town with medieval centre. Charter. *c.* 1170.

26. Plan of the new Brandenburg in East Germany. New Brandenburg dates from 1250.

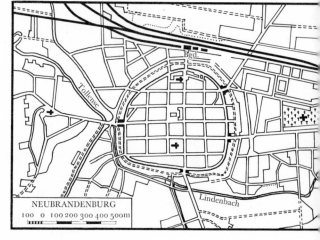

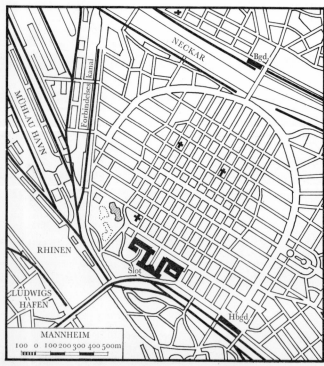

27. Capital town of a principality from the Baroque period (1607).